Introduction to Modern Web Technologies

Chapter 1: Introduction to Modern Web Development

An Overview of Web Technologies

The World Wide Web has become an integral part of our daily lives, and web technologies underpin its functionality and evolution. These technologies have evolved significantly since the early days of the internet, and they continue to shape the way we communicate, work, and access information. In this overview, we will delve into the fundamental web technologies that make the internet work, including protocols, languages, and frameworks.

1. Internet Protocols:

The foundation of the web lies in a set of protocols that enable communication and data exchange between devices and servers. Some of the most crucial internet protocols include:

a. HTTP/HTTPS: Hypertext Transfer Protocol (HTTP) and its secure counterpart, HTTPS, govern how information is transmitted over the web. HTTP is responsible for fetching web pages, images, and other resources from web servers, while HTTPS encrypts this data for secure transmission.

b. TCP/IP: The Transmission Control Protocol (TCP) and Internet Protocol (IP) are the backbone of internet communication. TCP manages data transmission and ensures reliability, while IP is responsible for routing and addressing.

c. DNS: The Domain Name System (DNS) translates human-readable domain names (e.g., www.example.com) into IP addresses, allowing browsers to locate web servers.

d. FTP: The File Transfer Protocol (FTP) is used for transferring files between a client and a server. It is commonly used for uploading website files or downloading software.

2. Web Markup Languages:

Web pages are created using markup languages that define the structure and content of a document. The most prominent markup languages are:

a. HTML: HyperText Markup Language (HTML) is the foundation of web pages. It structures content using elements like headings, paragraphs, links, and images. HTML5 introduced new features, such as audio and video support, that enrich the web experience.

b. CSS: Cascading Style Sheets (CSS) control the presentation and layout of web content. By defining colors, fonts, spacing, and positioning, CSS enhances the visual appeal of websites and ensures consistency across pages.

3. Client-Side Scripting:

Client-side scripting languages empower web browsers to interact with users and enhance the user experience. Notable client-side scripting languages include:

a. JavaScript: JavaScript is the most popular client-side scripting language. It enables interactive web features like dynamic content, form validation, and responsive design. Modern JavaScript libraries and frameworks like React and Angular simplify web development.

b. TypeScript: TypeScript is a superset of JavaScript that adds static typing and other features to improve code maintainability and developer productivity.

4. Server-Side Scripting:

Server-side scripting languages run on web servers, handling logic and data processing. They generate dynamic content, interact with databases, and manage user sessions. Key server-side scripting languages include:

a. PHP: PHP is widely used for server-side scripting, especially in the context of content management systems like WordPress. It can be embedded within HTML to create dynamic web pages.

b. Python: Python is a versatile language that is increasingly used for web development. Frameworks like Django and Flask make it easy to build web applications.

c. Ruby: Ruby on Rails is a popular framework for building web applications. It follows a convention over configuration (CoC) and don't repeat yourself (DRY) philosophy to enhance developer productivity.

d. Node.js: Node.js is a runtime environment that allows developers to use JavaScript for server-side scripting. It's known for its speed and scalability, making it a choice for real-time applications and microservices.

5. Web Frameworks:

Web development frameworks provide a structured way to build web applications, streamlining the development process. Some notable web frameworks include:

a. Ruby on Rails: This framework follows the Model-View-Controller (MVC) pattern, simplifying the development of database-driven web applications.

b. Django: Django, a Python framework, emphasizes a clean and pragmatic design. It includes an ORM (Object-Relational Mapping) system and follows the DRY principle.

c. Express.js: Express.js is a minimalist Node.js framework that is highly extensible and used for building web APIs and microservices.

d. Angular, React, and Vue: These front-end frameworks enable the creation of single-page applications with interactive user interfaces. Angular and React are maintained by Google and Facebook, respectively, while Vue.js is known for its simplicity and flexibility.

6. Databases:

Databases store and manage web application data. Several types of databases are used in web development, including:

a. Relational Databases: Examples include MySQL, PostgreSQL, and Microsoft SQL Server. They use structured tables to store data and support complex queries.

b. NoSQL Databases: These databases, such as MongoDB and Cassandra, are suitable for unstructured or semi-structured data and offer scalability and flexibility.

c. In-Memory Databases: Redis and Memcached are in-memory databases that provide fast data access, making them ideal for caching and real-time applications.

7. Web Servers:

Web servers are software that respond to incoming HTTP requests by serving web pages and resources. Popular web servers include:

a. Apache: Apache is one of the most widely used web servers, known for its reliability and extensibility.

b. Nginx: Nginx is acclaimed for its speed and efficiency, making it a common choice for serving static files, load balancing, and proxying.

8. Cloud Computing:

Cloud computing platforms like Amazon Web Services (AWS), Google Cloud Platform (GCP), and Microsoft Azure provide infrastructure and services that facilitate web application deployment, scalability, and management.

9. Web Security:

Web security is of utmost importance. Technologies such as SSL/TLS for encrypting data, Web Application Firewalls (WAFs) for protecting against threats, and secure coding practices play a crucial role in keeping web applications and data safe.

10. APIs and Web Services:

Application Programming Interfaces (APIs) allow different software systems to communicate with each other. Web services, including RESTful and SOAP services, enable data exchange and integration between web applications.

In conclusion, web technologies have evolved and diversified over the years, resulting in a rich ecosystem that empowers developers to create a wide range of web applications and services. Understanding these technologies is essential for anyone involved in web development, from creating simple web pages to building complex, data-driven applications. As the web continues to evolve, staying current with the latest developments in web technologies is vital for both seasoned professionals and newcomers to the field.

The Importance of Staying Current: Navigating the Ever-Changing Landscape

In an era marked by rapid technological advancements, shifting societal paradigms, and evolving industry trends, the importance of staying current cannot be overstated. Whether in the realm of technology, business, education, or personal development, staying current is vital for individuals and organizations alike. This article delves into the significance of keeping up with the times and offers insights into how to effectively do so.

1. Adaptation in a Fast-Paced World:

The world today is characterized by unprecedented levels of change. Technological innovations are occurring at a breakneck speed, industries are being disrupted, and global events can reshape the landscape overnight. To thrive in this dynamic environment, individuals and organizations must be able to adapt swiftly. Staying current ensures that you are equipped to adapt to new challenges and opportunities as they arise.

2. Professional Relevance:

In a highly competitive job market, professional relevance is a cornerstone of career success. Keeping up with the latest trends, tools, and skills in your field not only makes you a more attractive candidate to employers but also empowers you to excel in your current role. Irrelevant skills and knowledge can quickly lead to stagnation, hindering career advancement.

3. Innovation and Creativity:

Staying current is a catalyst for innovation and creativity. Exposure to new ideas, technologies, and methodologies sparks creativity and allows you to envision novel solutions to existing problems. Innovation is a driving force in business and society, and those who remain current are more likely to be at the forefront of groundbreaking developments.

4. Enhanced Decision-Making:

Sound decision-making relies on access to up-to-date information. Whether it's a business executive evaluating market trends, a student choosing a career path, or a healthcare provider making a medical diagnosis, staying current with the latest data and insights is imperative. Informed decisions are more likely to be successful.

5. Learning and Growth:

Continuous learning and personal growth are foundational principles for self-improvement. Staying current offers the opportunity to expand your knowledge base and skillset, leading to personal and professional growth. Lifelong learners are more adaptable, resilient, and better positioned to achieve their goals.

6. Business Competitiveness:

For organizations, staying current is a matter of survival. In today's business environment, companies that fail to adapt to changing customer preferences, market dynamics, and technological shifts risk obsolescence. Staying current ensures that a business remains competitive, responsive, and innovative.

7. Risk Mitigation:

Staying current is a form of risk mitigation. For instance, in cybersecurity, staying current with the latest threat intelligence is essential to protect systems and data from evolving threats. In investments, staying informed about financial markets and economic trends helps manage investment risk. Whether personal or professional, staying current can help identify and mitigate risks.

8. Technological Advancement:

Technology is the driving force behind many of the changes we experience today. Staying current with technological advancements is crucial, not only for tech professionals but for anyone. From the way we work and communicate to how we access information and perform daily tasks, technology impacts every aspect of our lives.

9. Digital Literacy:

Digital literacy is increasingly important as more aspects of life move online. Staying current with digital tools and platforms ensures that you can navigate the digital landscape effectively, from using online services to protecting your digital identity.

10. Global Connectivity:

The world is more interconnected than ever, with information and ideas flowing across borders. Staying current with global events, cultural trends, and international issues allows individuals and organizations to engage with a global audience and remain culturally sensitive and inclusive.

How to Stay Current:

The importance of staying current is evident, but the real challenge lies in how to achieve it effectively. Here are some strategies to help you stay current:

1. Continuous Learning:

Make learning a habit. Enroll in courses, attend workshops, read books, and stay updated with relevant publications in your field. Online learning platforms, such as Coursera, edX, and Khan Academy, offer a plethora of courses on various subjects.

2. Networking:

Engage in professional networks, both in-person and online. Join industry-specific groups, attend conferences, and participate in webinars. Networking allows you to tap into the collective knowledge of your peers.

3. News and Media Consumption:

Stay informed through news outlets, podcasts, and social media. Follow reputable sources for the latest updates in your field, but also be mindful of bias and misinformation.

4. Mentoring and Coaching:

Mentors and coaches can offer valuable insights and guidance. Seek out experienced individuals in your industry who can help you navigate the evolving landscape.

5. Skill Building:

Identify the skills that are in demand in your industry and work on acquiring or improving them. Online courses and certifications can help you gain relevant skills.

6. Embrace Change:

Be open to change and new opportunities. Embracing change rather than resisting it can help you adapt more quickly.

7. Cross-Disciplinary Learning:

Explore adjacent fields and industries to gain a broader perspective. Sometimes, innovations and ideas from other domains can be applied to your own.

8. Critical Thinking:

Develop critical thinking skills to evaluate information, sift through the noise, and discern what is genuinely valuable. Not all information is equally important, and critical thinking helps you focus on what matters.

9. Time Management:

Effectively managing your time is crucial when trying to stay current. Allocate dedicated time for learning and staying updated, and prioritize it alongside other commitments.

10. Reflection:

Regularly assess your skills, knowledge, and goals. Reflect on whether your current path aligns with your aspirations and adjust as needed.

In a world that is constantly evolving, the importance of staying current cannot be overstated. From personal growth and career success to business competitiveness and societal contribution, staying current is the key to navigating an ever-changing landscape. By adopting a proactive approach to learning, embracing change, and continuously seeking new knowledge and skills, individuals and organizations can thrive in this dynamic and fast-paced world. Staying current is not merely an option; it is a necessity for those who aspire to excel and make a meaningful impact in their respective fields.

Front-End vs. Back-End Development

Front-end and back-end development are two fundamental aspects of web development, each with its own unique role and set of skills. These roles work in tandem to create a seamless web experience. Understanding the differences between front-end and back-end development is crucial for anyone considering a career in web development or seeking to collaborate with web developers. In this overview, we'll explore the distinctions, responsibilities, and technologies associated with both front-end and back-end development.

Front-End Development:

Front-end development, also known as client-side development, focuses on the user interface and user experience (UI/UX) of a website or web application. Front-end developers are responsible for creating the visual elements that users interact with directly.

1. Responsibilities:

Front-end developers have a range of responsibilities, including:

- Creating the User Interface (UI): Designing and developing the layout, structure, and visual components of a web page or application, ensuring it's visually appealing and user-friendly.

- Implementing User Experience (UX) Design: Translating UX design concepts into functional and interactive elements, such as navigation menus, buttons, forms, and animations.
- Coding with HTML, CSS, and JavaScript: Using HTML (Hypertext Markup Language) for content structure, CSS (Cascading Style Sheets) for styling and layout, and JavaScript for adding interactivity and dynamic behavior to web pages.
- Responsive Design: Ensuring that websites are accessible and functional on various devices and screen sizes by implementing responsive design techniques.
- Cross-Browser Compatibility: Making sure web content displays and functions consistently across different web browsers and platforms.

2. Key Technologies:

Front-end development primarily involves the following technologies:

- HTML (Hypertext Markup Language): The standard markup language used for creating the structure and content of web pages.
- CSS (Cascading Style Sheets): Used for defining the visual styles, layout, and formatting of web content.
- JavaScript: A versatile scripting language used to create dynamic and interactive elements on a webpage, such as form validation, animations, and user interface enhancements.

- Front-End Frameworks: Libraries and frameworks like React, Angular, and Vue.js streamline the development of interactive web applications.
- Responsive Design Tools: CSS frameworks and media queries are employed for creating websites that adapt to various screen sizes and devices.

Back-End Development:

Back-end development, often referred to as server-side development, focuses on the behind-the-scenes operations of a website or web application. Back-end developers create the server, database, and application logic that enable front-end functionality and user interactions.

1. Responsibilities:

Back-end developers handle various crucial responsibilities, including:

- Server Configuration and Management: Setting up and managing the server where the web application is hosted.
- Database Management: Designing and maintaining the database systems that store data, such as user accounts, content, and application information.
- Application Logic: Creating the core functionality of the web application, which includes handling user authentication, data processing, and managing user interactions.
- API (Application Programming Interface) Development: Creating APIs that allow the front-end and back-end to communicate, enabling the exchange of data and information between the two.
- Security: Implementing security measures to protect user data and the web application from potential threats and vulnerabilities.

2. Key Technologies:

Back-end development relies on a variety of technologies and programming languages, including:

- Server-Side Programming Languages: Popular languages like Python, Ruby, Java, PHP, and Node.js are used for writing the server-side code.
- Databases: Back-end developers work with databases like MySQL, PostgreSQL, MongoDB, and SQL Server to store, retrieve, and manage data.
- Web Frameworks: Frameworks such as Ruby on Rails, Django, Express.js, and Laravel provide a structured way to build web applications and APIs.
- Server Management Tools: Tools like Apache, Nginx, and cloud platforms (e.g., AWS, Google Cloud, and Azure) are used for hosting and server management.
- API Development Tools: Creating RESTful or GraphQL APIs for front-end integration with tools like Express.js, Flask, or Spring Boot.

Front-End vs. Back-End Collaboration:

Front-end and back-end developers often collaborate to create a fully functional web application. The separation of responsibilities allows for efficient teamwork and specialization:

- Front-end developers work closely with designers to bring visual concepts to life. They interact with back-end developers to integrate user interfaces with the back-end logic, often via APIs.
- Back-end developers focus on the data and server-side processes, providing the necessary infrastructure for the front-end to operate. They

work with front-end developers to ensure that data is properly transmitted and processed.

Full-Stack Development:

In addition to front-end and back-end development, some developers specialize in full-stack development. Full-stack developers have expertise in both front-end and back-end technologies, allowing them to work on all aspects of a web application, from the user interface to the server and database.

Conclusion:

Front-end and back-end development are distinct yet interdependent components of web development. While front-end developers create the user interface and user experience, back-end developers build the infrastructure that supports the application's functionality. Collaboration between front-end and back-end developers is essential to create a cohesive and functional web application. Whether you're pursuing a career in web development or seeking to understand the development process, knowing the differences between front-end and back-end development is fundamental to successful web project execution.

Chapter 2: Development Environment Setup

Essential Tools and Software

Setting up a development environment is a crucial step for any software developer, as it provides the necessary tools and software to create, test, and deploy applications efficiently. The choice of tools and software may vary depending on the specific type of development you're engaged in (e.g., web, mobile, data science), but here's a general guide to essential tools and software for a well-rounded development environment setup:

1. Integrated Development Environment (IDE):

An integrated development environment is a software application that provides comprehensive features for coding, debugging, and building applications. The choice of IDE often depends on the programming language or framework you are using. Here are some popular IDEs for various purposes:

- Visual Studio Code (VS Code): A highly extensible, open-source code editor developed by Microsoft. It supports a wide range of programming languages and offers a vast library of extensions.
- Eclipse: A popular IDE for Java development, but it also supports various other programming languages through plugins.
- PyCharm: A powerful IDE for Python development, offering features like intelligent code completion and in-depth code analysis.
- IntelliJ IDEA: An IDE for Java, Kotlin, and other JVM-based languages with strong support for web and mobile development.

- Xcode: Essential for iOS and macOS development, providing tools for Swift and Objective-C.

2. Version Control System:

Version control systems help you track changes to your code, collaborate with others, and roll back to previous versions when needed. Git is the most widely used version control system, and you can choose from various hosting platforms like GitHub, GitLab, or Bitbucket to store your repositories.

3. Package Managers:

Package managers allow you to manage dependencies, libraries, and tools used in your projects. The choice of package manager depends on your development environment:

- npm (Node Package Manager): For managing JavaScript packages in Node.js and front-end development.
- pip: For Python package management.
- Composer: Used in PHP development for managing PHP packages and libraries.
- Bundler: Essential for managing Ruby gems in Ruby on Rails applications.

4. Text Editor:

A lightweight text editor is handy for quick edits and viewing code files. While many developers use their IDEs for text editing, a standalone text editor can be useful. Some popular options include Notepad++ (Windows), Sublime Text, and Atom.

5. Command-Line Tools:

Familiarity with command-line tools is important for tasks like running scripts, managing your development environment, and interacting with version control systems.

On Windows, consider installing Git Bash or Windows Subsystem for Linux (WSL) to access Unix-like command-line utilities.

6. Database Management Tools:

Database management tools facilitate database development, management, and querying. The choice of tool depends on the type of database you are working with:

- phpMyAdmin: A web-based tool for managing MySQL databases.
- pgAdmin: A graphical tool for PostgreSQL.
- DBeaver: Supports various databases and provides a unified interface for managing them.

7. Web Browsers:

Web development requires testing your applications in various browsers. You should have the latest versions of popular browsers like Google Chrome, Mozilla Firefox, Microsoft Edge, and Safari for testing and debugging.

8. Virtualization and Containerization:

Virtualization and containerization technologies are crucial for isolating development environments and simulating different server environments. Tools like Docker and virtual machines (e.g., VirtualBox) are invaluable for this purpose.

9. Development Frameworks and Libraries:

Depending on your area of development, you'll need specific frameworks, libraries, and SDKs. Here are some common examples:

- React and Angular: Popular front-end libraries for building user interfaces.
- Express.js: A web application framework for Node.js.
- Spring Boot: For building Java-based web applications.

- Django and Flask: Python web frameworks.
- Android Studio: For Android mobile app development.
- Xamarin: For cross-platform mobile app development using C#.
- Unity: A game development platform.

10. Testing and Debugging Tools:

Tools for testing and debugging are essential to ensure the quality and reliability of your code. Examples include JUnit for Java, Jest for JavaScript, and Pytest for Python.

11. Collaboration and Communication Tools:

For collaborative development and communication with teams and clients, consider tools like Slack, Microsoft Teams, or project management tools like Jira and Trello.

12. Cloud Services:

Cloud services such as Amazon Web Services (AWS), Microsoft Azure, and Google Cloud Platform (GCP) offer cloud infrastructure and services for deploying and scaling applications.

13. Text Editor Plugins and Extensions:

Depending on your choice of text editor or IDE, you can enhance your development environment with plugins or extensions that provide additional features and support for various languages and frameworks.

Remember that your specific development environment setup may vary based on your project requirements and personal preferences. Regularly updating and maintaining your tools and software is essential to keep your development environment efficient and secure. As technology evolves, staying current with the latest tools and best practices is crucial for a successful career in software development.

Version Control with Git

Version control with Git is a fundamental aspect of modern software development. Git is a distributed version control system that helps developers track changes in their code, collaborate with others, and manage software projects effectively. In this overview, we'll explore the key concepts and commands related to Git version control.

1. Git Basics:

Git is based on a few fundamental concepts:

- Repository (Repo): A Git repository is a directory where your project and version control data are stored.
- Commit: A commit is a snapshot of your project at a specific point in time. Each commit represents a set of changes you've made.
- Branch: A branch is a parallel line of development. You can create branches to work on new features or bug fixes without affecting the main project.
- Master (Main) Branch: The default branch in a Git repository is often called "master" or "main." It represents the latest stable version of the project.
- Remote Repository: A remote repository is hosted on a server, such as GitHub, GitLab, or Bitbucket. It allows multiple developers to collaborate and share their work.

2. Git Commands:

Here are some of the most common Git commands you'll use:

- git init: Initializes a new Git repository in your project directory.

- git clone [repository URL]: Creates a copy of a remote repository on your local machine.
- git add [file]: Stages changes for the next commit. You can also use git add . to stage all changes.
- git commit -m "[your message]": Commits the staged changes with a descriptive message.
- git pull: Fetches and merges changes from a remote repository into your local branch.
- git push: Pushes your local commits to a remote repository.
- git branch: Lists all branches in your repository.
- git checkout [branch]: Switches to the specified branch.
- git merge [branch]: Merges changes from one branch into the current branch.
- git log: Shows a history of commits in the current branch.
- git status: Displays the status of your working directory and staged changes.
- git diff: Compares changes between the working directory and the last commit.

3. Git Workflow:

The typical Git workflow involves creating a branch, making changes, committing those changes, and then merging them back into the main branch. Here's an example workflow:

Start by creating a new branch for your feature or bug fix: git checkout -b feature-branch.

Make changes to your code and stage them with git add.

Commit your changes with a descriptive message: git commit -m "Add new feature."

Push your branch to the remote repository: git push origin feature-branch.

Create a pull request or merge request (depending on your platform) to propose your changes for review and integration.

Reviewers can provide feedback, and once the changes are approved, merge the branch into the main branch.

After the branch is merged, you can delete it both locally and remotely: git branch -d feature-branch and git push origin --delete feature-branch.

4. Remote Collaboration:

Git enables remote collaboration on software projects. Platforms like GitHub, GitLab, and Bitbucket are commonly used to host Git repositories and facilitate collaboration. Developers can clone the repository, create branches, make changes, and then submit pull requests for review. Collaborators can comment on the code, and once changes are accepted, they can be merged into the main branch.

5. Git Best Practices:

To make the most of Git, consider the following best practices:

- Write meaningful commit messages that explain the purpose of the changes.
- Keep commits small and focused on a single task or feature.
- Pull and merge changes from the main branch regularly to avoid conflicts.
- Use branches for different features or bug fixes to isolate changes.

- Review and test code before merging it into the main branch.
- Keep your Git history clean by using tools like rebase to squash and reorganize commits.
- Regularly push your changes to the remote repository to avoid data loss.

6. Git Hosting Services:

Several popular Git hosting services are widely used for hosting repositories:

- GitHub: Offers a web-based interface for Git repositories and is commonly used for open-source projects.
- GitLab: Provides both a self-hosted option and a cloud-based service, with strong CI/CD integration.
- Bitbucket: Offers Git and Mercurial repository hosting with JIRA integration.

7. Git GUI Tools:

While Git is primarily command-line driven, there are also graphical user interface (GUI) tools available for those who prefer a visual interface. Some popular Git GUI tools include GitKraken, Sourcetree, and GitHub Desktop.

In conclusion, Git is an essential tool for modern software development. It enables version control, collaboration, and project management, making it indispensable for developers working on projects of any size. By understanding the basic concepts and commands, developers can effectively use Git to track changes, collaborate with others, and maintain clean and organized codebases.

Chapter 3: HTML5 and CSS3

Creating Structured Web Content

In this chapter, we will delve into the fundamental concepts and techniques for creating structured web content using HTML5 and enhancing its presentation with CSS3. HTML5 and CSS3 are the building blocks of modern web development, allowing developers to create rich, interactive, and visually appealing web pages. Let's explore the key elements and principles of these technologies.

1. Introduction to HTML5:

HTML5 is the latest version of Hypertext Markup Language, the standard markup language for creating web pages. It introduces several new features and elements that enable the creation of structured and semantically meaningful content. Some key HTML5 elements include:

- <!DOCTYPE html>: The document type declaration specifies the document type and version being used. In HTML5, it is simpler and more standardized.
- <html>: The root element that contains all other elements on the web page.
- <head>: Contains metadata about the document, such as the page title and links to external resources like stylesheets and scripts.
- <meta>: Provides metadata, such as character encoding and author information.
- <title>: Sets the title of the web page, which appears in the browser's tab or window.
- <link>: Specifies external resources, such as stylesheets, to be used by the web page.

- <script>: Embeds or references JavaScript code.
- <body>: Contains the visible content of the web page, including text, images, and multimedia.
- <header>, <nav>, <main>, <article>, <section>, <aside>, and <footer>: These elements are used to structure the content of the page and provide semantic meaning to its various sections.

2. HTML5 Semantic Elements:

HTML5 introduces semantic elements that help describe the meaning of content within the structure of a web page. Using these elements not only enhances accessibility but also improves search engine optimization (SEO). Some of the key semantic elements are:

- <header>: Represents introductory content or a set of navigational links.
- <nav>: Defines a navigation menu for the document or a part of the document.
- <main>: Represents the main content of the document.
- <article>: Encloses an independent, self-contained composition, such as a blog post or news article.
- <section>: Represents a thematic grouping of content, often containing a heading.
- <aside>: Contains content that is tangentially related to the content around it.
- <footer>: Represents a footer for its nearest ancestor section or block.

3. HTML5 Forms:

HTML5 introduces new input types and attributes for creating forms that are easier to use and more interactive. Some of the commonly used form elements include:

- <input type="text"> for single-line text input.

- <input type="password"> for password input.
- <input type="email"> for email input with built-in validation.
- <input type="number"> for numeric input with built-in validation.
- <input type="date"> for date selection.
- <textarea> for multiline text input.
- <select> for dropdown menus.
- <button> for custom buttons or form submission.

4. Introduction to CSS3:

Cascading Style Sheets (CSS) is used to control the presentation and layout of HTML elements. CSS3 is the latest version of CSS and brings new features and capabilities for designing visually appealing web pages. Key features of CSS3 include:

- Selectors: CSS3 introduces new selectors, such as attribute selectors, structural pseudo-classes, and more, to precisely target elements.
- Box Model: CSS3 provides more control over element sizing and layout, including the box-sizing property.
- Flexbox: The Flexbox layout model simplifies complex layouts and improves the alignment of elements.
- Grid Layout: The CSS Grid Layout enables two-dimensional layout control, which is especially useful for creating complex grids.
- Transitions and Animations: CSS3 allows smooth transitions and animations to enhance user experience.

5. CSS3 Properties:

CSS3 introduces a wide range of properties for styling web content, including:

- border-radius: Rounds the corners of elements.
- box-shadow: Adds shadows to elements.
- gradient backgrounds: Create gradient backgrounds with linear-gradient and radial-gradient.
- text-shadow: Adds shadows to text.
- transform: Apply 2D and 3D transformations to elements.
- transition: Specify transitions for smooth animations.
- animation: Create keyframe-based animations.

6. Responsive Web Design:

Responsive web design is the practice of creating web pages that adapt to various screen sizes and devices. CSS3 plays a vital role in responsive design by using media queries to apply different styles based on the device's characteristics, such as width and resolution.

7. Best Practices:

To create structured web content effectively, consider the following best practices:

- Use semantic HTML5 elements to provide meaning to your content.
- Organize your HTML and CSS code by following a consistent naming convention and indentation.
- Optimize images and multimedia elements for faster page loading.
- Validate your HTML and CSS to ensure standards compliance.
- Test your web pages on different browsers and devices to ensure cross-browser compatibility.
- Keep your code clean and maintainable to facilitate collaboration and future updates.

Conclusion:

HTML5 and CSS3 are the cornerstones of modern web development. By using semantic HTML5 elements to structure content and leveraging the advanced styling and layout capabilities of CSS3, web developers can create structured and visually appealing web pages that provide a rich and accessible user experience across various devices and screen sizes. Embracing these technologies and best practices is essential for staying current in the dynamic field of web development.

Responsive Web Design Techniques

Responsive web design is a critical approach in modern web development, as it ensures that websites and web applications look and function well on a variety of devices and screen sizes, including desktops, laptops, tablets, and smartphones. Here are some key techniques and best practices for implementing responsive web design:

1. Fluid Grid Layout:

Use a fluid grid layout as the foundation of your design. This means using relative units like percentages instead of fixed units like pixels for defining widths and positions. For example, you can set a container to be 100% wide, and the contained elements can be specified in percentages as well.

css

```css
.container {
  width: 100%;
}
```

```css
.column {
  width: 33.33%;
}
```

2. Media Queries:
Media queries allow you to apply specific CSS styles based on the characteristics of the device or viewport, such as screen width, height, or orientation. This is the core technique for responsive design.
css

```css
/* CSS for screens with a maximum width of 768px */
@media (max-width: 768px) {
  /* Adjust styles for smaller screens */
}

/* CSS for screens with a minimum width of 1024px */
@media (min-width: 1024px) {
  /* Adjust styles for larger screens */
}
```

3. Flexible Images and Media:
Images and other media should be flexible and adapt to different screen sizes. Use the max-width: 100% style to ensure that images don't overflow their containing elements. Additionally, consider using the picture element or srcset attribute to serve different image sizes based on the device's resolution.
css

```css
img {
```

```css
  max-width: 100%;
}
```

4. CSS Flexbox and Grid Layout:
CSS Flexbox and Grid Layout are powerful tools for creating flexible and responsive layouts. Flexbox is excellent for one-dimensional layouts, while Grid Layout is designed for two-dimensional layouts. These technologies simplify the creation of complex responsive designs.

5. Mobile-First Design:
A mobile-first approach involves designing for mobile devices first and then progressively enhancing the design for larger screens. This ensures that the site is optimized for the smallest screens, and additional features are added for larger ones.

6. Breakpoints:
Breakpoints are specific screen widths where you make design adjustments. Common breakpoints might be set at 320px (small mobile), 768px (tablet), and 1024px (small desktop). However, you can add more breakpoints as needed.

7. Typography and Font Size:
Use relative units like em or rem for defining font sizes and line heights. This allows text to scale appropriately with the screen size.

css

```css
body {
  font-size: 16px;
}

@media (max-width: 768px) {
```

```css
  body {
    font-size: 14px;
  }
}
```

8. Viewport Meta Tag:
Include a viewport meta tag in your HTML to control the viewport dimensions and scaling. This is crucial for ensuring that websites are displayed correctly on mobile devices.
html

```html
<meta name="viewport" content="width=device-width, initial-scale=1">
```

9. Testing:
Regularly test your responsive designs on various devices, browsers, and screen sizes. Consider using browser developer tools, online emulators, or real devices for testing.

10. Progressive Enhancement:
Progressive enhancement is the practice of delivering a basic, usable website to all users and then progressively enhancing it with additional features for users with more capable devices and browsers. This ensures that the site works for everyone, regardless of their technology limitations.

11. Performance Optimization:
Optimize the performance of your responsive design by using techniques like lazy loading for images, minimizing HTTP requests, and leveraging browser caching.

12. Accessibility:

Ensure your responsive design is accessible to all users, including those with disabilities. Use semantic HTML, provide alt text for images, and ensure that interactive elements are keyboard-friendly.

13. Device Testing:

Conduct testing on real devices to verify that your responsive design works as intended on a variety of platforms.

14. User Testing:

Gather feedback from actual users to identify issues with your responsive design and make necessary improvements.

15. Content Prioritization:

Consider what content is most important for mobile users and ensure that it is prominently displayed, while secondary content can be tucked away or shown differently on larger screens.

Responsive web design is an ongoing process that involves creating flexible layouts, optimizing performance, and providing an excellent user experience on various devices. By implementing these techniques and best practices, you can create web applications that adapt seamlessly to the diverse array of screens and devices in use today.

Chapter 4: JavaScript and ES6

JavaScript Fundamentals

JavaScript is a versatile and essential programming language for web development. In this chapter, we will explore the fundamental concepts and features of JavaScript, including the enhancements introduced in ECMAScript 6 (ES6). These concepts lay the foundation for creating dynamic and interactive web applications.

1. Introduction to JavaScript:

JavaScript is a high-level, dynamic, and interpreted programming language used to enhance web pages with interactivity and dynamic behavior. It is an integral part of web development, running in web browsers and on the server-side (Node.js). JavaScript enables developers to manipulate HTML and CSS, interact with users, and manage data.

2. Variables and Data Types:

JavaScript includes various data types, such as numbers, strings, booleans, objects, and arrays. You can declare variables using var, let, or const. ES6 introduced let and const for better variable scoping and immutability.

javascript

```
var name = "John";
let age = 30;
const isStudent = true;
```

3. Operators:

JavaScript provides operators for arithmetic, comparison, logical operations, and string concatenation. For example:

javascript

```javascript
let result = 10 + 5; // addition
let isGreater = 20 > 10; // comparison
let andOperator = true && false; // logical AND
let fullName = "John" + " Doe"; // string concatenation
```

4. Control Structures:
Control structures like if, else, switch, for, while, and do...while are used for decision-making and looping.
javascript

```javascript
if (condition) {
  // code to execute if condition is true
} else {
  // code to execute if condition is false
}

for (let i = 0; i < 5; i++) {
  // loop code
}
```

5. Functions:
Functions are blocks of code that can be reused. You can define functions using function or arrow (=>) notation in ES6.
javascript

```javascript
function add(a, b) {
  return a + b;
}
```

```javascript
const multiply = (a, b) => a * b;
```

6. Objects and Arrays:
Objects and arrays are important data structures in JavaScript. Objects store data in key-value pairs, while arrays store data in ordered lists.
javascript

```javascript
const person = {
  name: "Alice",
  age: 25
};

const colors = ["red", "green", "blue"];
```

7. Events and Event Handling:
JavaScript enables interaction with web pages by handling events like clicks, keypresses, and form submissions. You can add event listeners to respond to events.
javascript

```javascript
const button = document.querySelector("#myButton");
button.addEventListener("click", () => {
  alert("Button clicked!");
});
```

8. DOM Manipulation:
The Document Object Model (DOM) represents the structure of web pages. JavaScript can manipulate the DOM to change or update elements dynamically.
javascript

```javascript
const element = document.getElementById("myElement");
element.innerHTML = "New content";
```

9. ES6 Features:
ECMAScript 6 (ES6) introduced several enhancements to JavaScript, making it more powerful and readable. Key ES6 features include:
- Arrow Functions: A more concise way to define functions.
- Template Literals: Easier string interpolation.
- Destructuring: Extracting values from objects and arrays.
- Spread and Rest Operators: Managing arrays and function parameters.
- Classes: A new way to create and manage objects with inheritance.
- Promises: Improved handling of asynchronous operations.
- Modules: A standardized system for organizing and loading JavaScript code.

10. Error Handling:
JavaScript provides mechanisms for error handling, including try...catch blocks, which allow you to handle exceptions gracefully.
javascript

```
try {
  // code that may throw an error
} catch (error) {
  // handle the error
}
```

11. Asynchronous JavaScript:

Asynchronous programming is essential for handling tasks like network requests. JavaScript uses callbacks, promises, and async/await to manage asynchronous operations.

javascript

```
fetch("https://api.example.com/data")
  .then(response => response.json())
  .then(data => console.log(data))
  .catch(error => console.error(error));
```

12. Best Practices:

When working with JavaScript, consider these best practices:

- Use meaningful variable and function names.
- Follow coding conventions and style guides (e.g., ES6, Airbnb, or Google JavaScript style guides).
- Comment your code to explain complex logic or functions.
- Minimize the use of global variables to avoid variable name collisions.
- Test your code thoroughly to catch and fix bugs early.

Conclusion:

JavaScript is a dynamic and versatile programming language used extensively in web development. Understanding JavaScript fundamentals, including data types, control structures, functions, and ES6 enhancements, is crucial for creating interactive and dynamic web applications. By mastering these concepts and following best practices, you'll be well-equipped to build responsive and engaging web experiences.

Asynchronous programming

Asynchronous programming is a crucial concept in modern software development, allowing programs to execute multiple tasks concurrently without blocking the main thread of execution. Asynchronous operations are essential for handling time-consuming tasks like I/O operations, network requests, and user interactions in a non-blocking manner. In this overview, we'll explore the basics of asynchronous programming, including key techniques and best practices.

1. Synchronous vs. Asynchronous Execution:

In synchronous programming, tasks are executed one after the other, and the program waits for each task to complete before moving on to the next one. This can lead to performance issues and unresponsiveness in applications.

In contrast, asynchronous programming allows multiple tasks to run concurrently without blocking the main program execution. This results in more responsive applications and improved performance.

2. Callbacks:

Callbacks are a common way to implement asynchronous behavior in JavaScript. A callback is a function that is passed as an argument to another function and is executed after the completion of an asynchronous operation. Here's a simple example using a callback for asynchronous file reading:

javascript

```javascript
const fs = require('fs');

fs.readFile('file.txt', 'utf8', (err, data) => {
  if (err) {
```

```javascript
    console.error(err);
    return;
  }
  console.log(data);
});
```

3. Promises:

Promises are a more structured and readable way to handle asynchronous operations. A promise represents a value that might not be available yet but will be at some point in the future. Promises have three states: pending, fulfilled, or rejected.

javascript

```javascript
const fetchData = () => {
  return new Promise((resolve, reject) => {
    // Simulate an asynchronous operation
    setTimeout(() => {
      const data = 'Async data';
      resolve(data); // Operation succeeded
      // or reject(error) if it fails
    }, 2000);
  });
};

fetchData()
  .then(data => {
    console.log(data);
  })
  .catch(error => {
    console.error(error);
  });
```

4. async/await:
The async/await syntax, introduced in ES6 (ECMAScript 2017), simplifies asynchronous code even further. The async keyword defines an asynchronous function, and the await keyword is used within an async function to pause execution until a promise is resolved.
javascript

```javascript
async function fetchData() {
  // Simulate an asynchronous operation
  return new Promise(resolve => {
    setTimeout(() => {
      resolve('Async data');
    }, 2000);
  });
}

async function main() {
  try {
    const data = await fetchData();
    console.log(data);
  } catch (error) {
    console.error(error);
  }
}

main();
```

5. Event Loop:
In JavaScript, the event loop is responsible for managing asynchronous operations. It continuously checks the

message queue for pending events or tasks and executes them one by one. This allows JavaScript to remain single-threaded while handling multiple asynchronous operations.

6. Threading and Parallelism:

JavaScript is single-threaded, which means it can execute only one operation at a time. However, modern web APIs and environments, such as web workers in browsers, provide limited support for multi-threading and parallelism to perform computationally intensive tasks in the background.

7. Error Handling:

Proper error handling is crucial in asynchronous programming. Using try...catch blocks or handling errors with promises and async/await ensures that errors are captured and handled gracefully, preventing application crashes.

8. Best Practices:

- Use promises and async/await to write clean and readable asynchronous code.
- Avoid deep nesting of callbacks (known as "callback hell") by using promises and async/await.
- Be mindful of error handling to prevent uncaught exceptions.
- Understand the event loop and the non-blocking nature of JavaScript.
- Profile and optimize your code to ensure efficient use of resources.

9. Use Cases:

Asynchronous programming is essential for various scenarios, including:

- Fetching data from external APIs.
- Reading and writing files.

- Making network requests.
- Performing database operations.
- Handling user input and interactions.

In conclusion, asynchronous programming is a foundational concept in modern software development, enabling the creation of responsive and efficient applications. By using techniques like callbacks, promises, and async/await, developers can handle time-consuming tasks without blocking the main thread. Understanding the event loop and proper error handling are key to mastering asynchronous programming in JavaScript and other languages.

Chapter 5: Front-End Frameworks

Introduction to Popular Frameworks

Front-end frameworks are a fundamental part of modern web development, providing tools and structures that make it easier to create responsive and dynamic web applications. In this chapter, we'll introduce you to some of the most popular front-end frameworks and discuss their key features and use cases.

1. Angular:

Angular, developed and maintained by Google, is a comprehensive front-end framework for building dynamic web applications. It offers features such as two-way data binding, dependency injection, and a robust component-based architecture. Key features of Angular include:

- TypeScript: Angular is written in TypeScript, a statically typed superset of JavaScript, which helps catch errors early and improve code quality.
- Component-Based Architecture: Angular applications are built by composing components that represent different parts of the user interface.
- Directives: Angular provides powerful directives for manipulating the DOM and creating dynamic templates.
- Dependency Injection: It has a built-in dependency injection system for managing application dependencies.
- RxJS: Angular leverages RxJS for handling asynchronous operations and event handling.

Angular is ideal for building complex web applications, including single-page applications (SPAs) and enterprise-grade software.

2. React:

React, maintained by Facebook, is a popular JavaScript library for building user interfaces. It focuses on creating reusable UI components and managing the view layer of web applications. Key features of React include:

- Virtual DOM: React uses a virtual representation of the DOM, which allows for efficient updates and improved performance.
- Component-Based: React applications are composed of reusable components that can be easily combined to create complex interfaces.
- Unidirectional Data Flow: Data flows in one direction, making it easier to manage and debug application state.
- React Native: React can be used to develop native mobile applications for both iOS and Android.

React is a versatile choice for creating user interfaces and can be integrated into existing projects.

3. Vue.js:

Vue.js is an open-source front-end framework known for its simplicity and ease of integration into projects. It offers a progressive framework, allowing developers to use as much or as little of its features as needed. Key features of Vue.js include:

- Virtual DOM: Similar to React, Vue.js uses a virtual DOM to optimize rendering.
- Component-Based: Vue.js applications are built using components, making it easy to maintain and scale.

- Two-Way Data Binding: Vue.js offers two-way data binding, simplifying data manipulation.
- Vue Router: A built-in routing library for creating single-page applications.
- Vuex: A state management library for managing application-wide state.

Vue.js is an excellent choice for both small and large-scale applications, offering a gentle learning curve for new developers.

4. Bootstrap:

Bootstrap is a popular open-source CSS framework developed by Twitter. It provides a set of CSS and JavaScript components, including grids, forms, buttons, and navigation, that make it easy to create responsive and visually appealing web interfaces. Key features of Bootstrap include:

- Responsive Grid System: A flexible grid system that adapts to different screen sizes.
- Component Library: Pre-designed UI components and styles that save development time.
- Customization: Bootstrap can be customized to match a project's design and branding.
- Community Support: A vast community and numerous templates, themes, and extensions are available.

Bootstrap is ideal for quickly prototyping and building visually consistent web applications.

5. SASS/SCSS:

SASS (Syntactically Awesome Style Sheets) and SCSS (Sassy CSS) are preprocessor scripting languages that extend the capabilities of regular CSS. They add features like variables, nesting, and mixins, making stylesheets more maintainable and easier to work with. Key features of SASS/SCSS include:

- Variables: Define reusable values for colors, fonts, and more.
- Nesting: Organize CSS rules within a nested structure, improving readability.
- Mixins: Reuse blocks of CSS, reducing duplication.
- Math Operations: Perform mathematical operations within stylesheets.

SASS/SCSS is a valuable tool for front-end developers and designers who want to write more efficient and organized CSS.

6. Material-UI:

Material-UI is a popular open-source library that implements Google's Material Design guidelines in React components. It provides a set of ready-to-use UI components that adhere to Material Design principles, making it easy to create modern, visually appealing web applications.

Conclusion:

Front-end frameworks and libraries play a pivotal role in modern web development, enabling developers to create responsive and feature-rich web applications. Each framework has its strengths and use cases, so the choice depends on the specific project requirements and developer preferences. Whether you're building a complex web application with Angular, a user interface with React, or enhancing your styles with SASS, these tools can help streamline development and improve the user experience.

Building Single-Page Applications

Building Single-Page Applications (SPAs) is a modern approach to web development that provides a seamless and responsive user experience. SPAs load a single HTML page and dynamically update the content as the user interacts with the application, eliminating the need for full-page refreshes. In this overview, we'll discuss the key concepts and techniques for building SPAs.

1. Understanding SPAs:

A Single-Page Application is characterized by the following features:

- Single HTML Page: SPAs load a single HTML page initially and update its content dynamically, typically using JavaScript.
- Client-Side Routing: SPAs use client-side routing to handle navigation within the application, changing the URL without triggering a full-page reload.
- AJAX and API Calls: Data is loaded asynchronously using AJAX or Fetch API calls, which update the content without refreshing the page.
- Smooth Transitions: SPAs often use animations and transitions to create a smooth and engaging user experience.

2. Advantages of SPAs:

SPAs offer several advantages, including:

- Faster User Experience: SPAs reduce the need for full-page reloads, resulting in faster load times and smoother interactions.
- Improved Responsiveness: SPAs provide a more responsive and app-like user experience, even on slow network connections.

- Reduced Server Load: Server-side resources are used more efficiently because only data is exchanged, not entire HTML pages.
- Enhanced Interactivity: SPAs allow for complex client-side interactivity and real-time updates.

3. Key Technologies for SPAs:

To build SPAs, you'll need to be familiar with the following technologies:

- HTML and CSS: These form the foundation for your application's structure and styling.
- JavaScript: JavaScript is essential for creating the dynamic behavior and interactions in your SPA. Libraries like React, Angular, or Vue are commonly used for building SPAs.
- Client-Side Routing: Implement client-side routing using libraries like React Router or Vue Router to manage navigation within your SPA.
- AJAX and APIs: Use AJAX, Fetch API, or libraries like Axios to make asynchronous requests to fetch and update data.
- State Management: SPAs often require state management solutions like Redux (for React), Vuex (for Vue), or the built-in state management of Angular.

4. SPA Architecture:

A typical SPA follows a structured architecture, which includes:

- Components: Break down your application into reusable components, each responsible for a specific part of the user interface.

- Routing: Implement client-side routing to handle navigation between different views or sections of your SPA.
- API Integration: Interact with server-side APIs to fetch and update data.
- State Management: Manage the application's state, including user data and application-wide settings.
- View Rendering: Render the views dynamically based on the application's state and user interactions.

5. SEO Considerations:

One challenge with SPAs is that search engine optimization (SEO) can be more complex due to the dynamic nature of the content. To improve SEO for SPAs:

- Use server-side rendering (SSR) to generate HTML on the server and send it to the client, making content more accessible to search engines.
- Implement dynamic meta tags and structured data to provide context to search engines.

6. Best Practices:

When building SPAs, consider the following best practices:

- Prioritize performance by optimizing asset delivery and reducing the initial load time.
- Implement client-side routing to create a user-friendly and intuitive navigation system.
- Focus on accessibility to ensure that your SPA is usable by everyone, including those with disabilities.
- Use lazy loading for components to reduce the initial load time and enhance the user experience.
- Implement code splitting to load only the code needed for the current view, improving performance.

7. Testing and Debugging:

Test your SPA thoroughly to ensure it works correctly across various browsers and devices. Debugging tools provided by browsers and developer extensions like React DevTools and Vue.js Devtools can help in diagnosing issues.

8. Deployment:

Deploy your SPA to a web server or hosting platform. Ensure that your server is configured to handle client-side routing correctly, and make use of content delivery networks (CDNs) for asset delivery.

Conclusion:

Single-Page Applications are a popular and effective approach for building modern web applications that provide a seamless, interactive, and responsive user experience. By understanding the core concepts and technologies associated with SPAs and following best practices, you can create web applications that meet the demands of today's users and provide a highly engaging and dynamic user experience.

Chapter 6: Back-End Development with Node.js

Server-Side JavaScript

1. Introduction to Node.js:
Node.js is an open-source, cross-platform runtime environment built on the V8 JavaScript engine. It enables developers to write server-side applications using JavaScript. Key features of Node.js include:

- Non-blocking I/O: Node.js uses an event-driven, non-blocking model, which makes it highly efficient for handling I/O-bound tasks.
- NPM (Node Package Manager): NPM is a package manager that provides access to a vast ecosystem of open-source libraries and modules.
- Single-Threaded: Node.js is single-threaded but supports concurrency through event loops, enabling it to handle multiple requests simultaneously.

2. Building Server Applications:
Node.js is well-suited for building various types of server applications, including:

- API Servers: Building RESTful APIs or GraphQL servers for web and mobile applications.
- Real-Time Applications: Developing real-time applications like chat applications, online gaming, and collaborative tools.
- Microservices: Creating microservices-based architectures for scalable and modular applications.
- IoT (Internet of Things): Handling communication between IoT devices and the cloud.
- Web Servers: Serving web pages and static assets.

3. Core Modules and NPM:

Node.js provides core modules for common tasks like file I/O, networking, and more. Additionally, the Node Package Manager (NPM) allows you to easily install, manage, and update third-party libraries and modules. You can use NPM to access thousands of packages to extend Node.js's capabilities.

4. Asynchronous Programming:

Node.js's event-driven architecture relies on callbacks to handle asynchronous operations. Understanding the use of callbacks, Promises, and async/await is crucial for writing non-blocking code and avoiding callback hell.

5. Express.js:

Express.js is a popular web application framework for Node.js. It simplifies the process of building robust and scalable web applications by providing a set of features, including routing, middleware, and template engines.

6. RESTful APIs:

Node.js is commonly used to create RESTful APIs. Using libraries like Express.js, you can define routes, handle HTTP methods (GET, POST, PUT, DELETE), and connect to databases to perform CRUD (Create, Read, Update, Delete) operations.

7. Database Integration:

Node.js can connect to various databases, including relational databases like MySQL and PostgreSQL, NoSQL databases like MongoDB, and in-memory databases like Redis. Libraries like Mongoose (for MongoDB) and Sequelize (for SQL databases) simplify database interactions.

8. Authentication and Authorization:

Implementing user authentication and authorization is a critical aspect of back-end development. Node.js can be used to integrate authentication methods like JWT (JSON Web Tokens) and OAuth.

9. WebSocket Communication:

Node.js is ideal for real-time applications and supports WebSocket communication. Libraries like Socket.io simplify real-time data exchange between the server and clients.

10. Performance and Scalability:

Node.js is known for its performance and scalability. Its non-blocking I/O model and event-driven architecture make it efficient for handling concurrent connections and I/O-bound tasks.

11. Testing and Debugging:

Node.js provides a range of tools for testing and debugging, including built-in tools like the Node.js Inspector and third-party tools like Mocha, Chai, and Jest for testing.

12. Deployment:

Deploying Node.js applications can be done on various platforms, including cloud services, dedicated servers, and containerization technologies like Docker. Proper configuration and load balancing are essential for scaling and ensuring high availability.

13. Security:

Node.js applications should be secured against common threats like injection attacks, Cross-Site Scripting (XSS), and Cross-Site Request Forgery (CSRF). Using security libraries like Helmet and following best practices is crucial.

14. Monitoring and Logging:

Implement monitoring and logging to track the health and performance of your application. Tools like New Relic, PM2, and Winston help in this regard.

15. Future of Node.js:

Node.js continues to evolve, with regular updates and improvements. Understanding its future trends and staying up-to-date with the latest features and practices is essential for effective back-end development.

Conclusion:

Node.js has revolutionized server-side development by allowing developers to use JavaScript across the full stack. With its non-blocking I/O, extensive ecosystem of libraries, and high performance, Node.js has become a top choice for building scalable and efficient server applications. By mastering Node.js, you can create robust, high-performing back-end systems to support a wide range of web and application requirements.

RESTful API Development

Representational State Transfer (REST) is an architectural style for designing networked applications. RESTful APIs (Application Programming Interfaces) are a way to implement the principles of REST for creating web services. In this overview, we'll discuss the fundamentals of RESTful API development.

1. Understanding REST:

REST is based on several principles:

- Stateless: Each request from a client to a server must contain all the information needed to understand and process the request. The server should not store any information about the client's state between requests.

- Client-Server: The client and server are separate entities that communicate over a stateless request-response protocol (usually HTTP).
- Uniform Interface: A consistent and uniform set of rules and constraints are used for interactions, including resources, HTTP methods, and status codes.
- Resource-Based: Resources are identified by URIs (Uniform Resource Identifiers) and are manipulated using standard HTTP methods like GET, POST, PUT, and DELETE.
- Representation: Resources can have multiple representations (e.g., JSON, XML, HTML). Clients interact with resources through their representations.

2. Key Concepts:
- Resources: In REST, everything is a resource. Resources can represent data entities like users, products, or articles. Each resource is identified by a unique URI.
- HTTP Methods: RESTful APIs use HTTP methods for CRUD (Create, Read, Update, Delete) operations on resources. Common methods include GET (retrieve data), POST (create data), PUT (update data), and DELETE (remove data).
- Uniform Resource Identifier (URI): URIs are used to identify resources. They should be meaningful and represent the resource they point to.
- Request and Response: Requests are made by clients to perform actions on resources. Responses from the server contain status codes and data representations.

3. Designing RESTful APIs:

To design effective RESTful APIs, consider these best practices:

- Use nouns for resource names in URIs (e.g., /products instead of /getListOfProducts).
- Use HTTP methods consistently for operations (GET for retrieval, POST for creation, PUT for updates, DELETE for removal).
- Use meaningful status codes in responses (e.g., 200 for success, 201 for resource creation, 404 for resource not found).
- Use proper versioning to maintain backward compatibility with clients.
- Keep URLs simple and avoid query parameters when possible. Use them for filtering and pagination.
- Use consistent naming conventions for resource attributes (e.g., camelCase or snake_case).

4. Authentication and Authorization:

Secure your RESTful API with authentication and authorization mechanisms. Common approaches include:

- Token-based Authentication: Using tokens like JSON Web Tokens (JWT) to authenticate clients.
- OAuth: For allowing third-party applications to access user data.
- API Keys: Providing a unique key for each client.

5. Data Serialization:

Use standard data serialization formats like JSON or XML to represent resources in responses. JSON is the most popular choice for its simplicity and readability.

6. Pagination:

For resource collections with many items, implement pagination to limit the number of results returned in a single response. Use query parameters like ?page=2&per_page=10 to allow clients to navigate large data sets.

7. Error Handling:

Implement consistent error handling and provide meaningful error responses with proper status codes (e.g., 400 for client errors, 500 for server errors).

8. Versioning:

Consider versioning your API to ensure backward compatibility as you make changes over time. Common versioning approaches include using a version number in the URI or via a header.

9. Documentation:

Provide comprehensive API documentation that explains available resources, their URIs, supported HTTP methods, and expected request and response formats. Tools like Swagger or OpenAPI can help automate the documentation process.

10. Testing and Debugging:

Thoroughly test your API using testing frameworks and tools. Debugging tools like Postman or Insomnia help in testing endpoints and troubleshooting issues.

11. Rate Limiting:

Implement rate limiting to control the number of requests clients can make to your API to prevent abuse and ensure fair usage.

12. Security:

Apply security best practices, such as input validation, to prevent common security vulnerabilities like SQL injection and Cross-Site Scripting (XSS).

13. Monitoring and Analytics:

Implement monitoring and analytics to track API usage, performance, and errors. Services like New Relic and Datadog can help in this regard.

14. Scaling and Load Balancing:

Plan for scalability and use load balancing to distribute incoming requests across multiple servers or instances to handle increased traffic.

15. Version Control:

Use version control systems like Git to manage the source code and configuration of your API.

16. Deploying and Hosting:

Choose a suitable hosting platform for deploying your RESTful API. Cloud providers like AWS, Azure, and Google Cloud offer scalable solutions.

Conclusion:

Building RESTful APIs is a fundamental part of modern web development. By following REST principles, designing meaningful URIs, using HTTP methods appropriately, and implementing secure authentication and authorization mechanisms, you can create robust and efficient APIs that enable effective communication between clients and servers. Thorough testing, monitoring, and documentation are key to ensuring the success of your API.

Chapter 7: Databases and Data Storage

Database Types and Best Practices

Databases play a vital role in storing, organizing, and retrieving data for web applications and systems. In this chapter, we will explore various types of databases and best practices for working with them in the context of web development.

1. Introduction to Databases:

Databases are systems for storing, managing, and retrieving structured data. They are essential for web applications to persist data, such as user information, content, and application settings. Common types of databases used in web development include:

- Relational Databases (RDBMS): Examples include MySQL, PostgreSQL, and SQLite. They store data in structured tables with predefined schemas.
- NoSQL Databases: These databases are non-relational and include document databases (e.g., MongoDB), key-value stores (e.g., Redis), column-family stores (e.g., Cassandra), and graph databases (e.g., Neo4j).

2. Choosing the Right Database:

Selecting the right type of database for your web application depends on factors like data structure, scalability, and performance requirements. Consider the following:

- Use relational databases for structured data with well-defined schemas and complex queries.

- Choose NoSQL databases when dealing with unstructured or semi-structured data and when scalability is a priority.
- Hybrid approaches that combine both types can be beneficial for certain applications.

3. Best Practices for Database Design:

Effective database design is crucial for performance, maintainability, and data integrity. Follow these best practices:

- Normalization: Organize data to minimize redundancy and improve data integrity by adhering to normalization principles.
- Indexes: Use indexes for frequently queried columns to speed up data retrieval. Be cautious with over-indexing, as it can impact write performance.
- Data Validation: Implement data validation and constraints to ensure data integrity and prevent data inconsistencies.
- Optimized Queries: Write efficient SQL or NoSQL queries by avoiding costly operations and optimizing data retrieval.

4. Data Modeling:

For relational databases, design your data model carefully by considering relationships, primary keys, foreign keys, and data types.

- Entity-Relationship Diagrams: Use ER diagrams to visualize your data model and relationships.
- Referential Integrity: Enforce referential integrity constraints to maintain data consistency.

5. Security and Authentication:

Implement robust security measures to protect your database:

- Authentication: Use strong authentication mechanisms and avoid storing passwords in plain text.
- Authorization: Set access controls to ensure that users have appropriate privileges.
- Encryption: Encrypt sensitive data both in transit and at rest.

6. Scalability:

Plan for scalability from the beginning. Choose databases that can scale horizontally or vertically, depending on your needs. Employ load balancing, sharding, and caching as appropriate.

7. Backups and Recovery:

Regularly back up your database and test the recovery process to ensure data can be restored in case of data loss or corruption.

8. Monitoring and Performance Tuning:

Set up monitoring tools to track database performance and identify bottlenecks. Continuously optimize queries, indexes, and database settings.

9. Error Handling:

Handle database errors gracefully by providing informative error messages and implementing retry mechanisms when applicable.

10. Data Migration:

Plan for data migration between database versions, especially in the case of schema changes or upgrades.

11. NoSQL Database Considerations:

For NoSQL databases, such as document databases or key-value stores, remember the following:

- Document databases are suitable for semi-structured data where flexibility is essential.

- Key-value stores are efficient for caching and session management.
- Column-family stores are appropriate for time-series or analytical data.
- Graph databases are designed for managing and querying highly connected data.

12. Caching:

Utilize caching solutions like Redis or Memcached to reduce database load and improve response times.

13. Testing and Development Environments:

Maintain separate testing and development environments to avoid accidental data corruption in production.

14. Disaster Recovery:

Create a disaster recovery plan that includes regular backups, redundancy, and geographic distribution for critical data.

15. Compliance and Regulations:

Adhere to data protection regulations and industry-specific compliance requirements (e.g., GDPR, HIPAA).

16. Data Privacy:

Respect user privacy and secure sensitive information. Minimize data collection to only what is necessary for your application.

Conclusion:

Databases are at the core of web application development, and proper database design and management are essential for data integrity, performance, and scalability. By following best practices for database design, security, scalability, and maintenance, you can ensure your web application's database system is robust and efficient, providing a solid foundation for your application to thrive.

Database Design

Database design is a critical aspect of building robust and efficient database systems for web applications. Proper database design ensures data integrity, performance, scalability, and ease of maintenance. In this overview, we'll explore key concepts and best practices for effective database design.

1. Define the Purpose and Requirements:
   - Start by understanding the purpose of your database. What kind of data will it store, and what are the requirements of your web application? This information will guide your design decisions.

2. Choose the Right Database Type:
   - Decide whether you need a relational database (RDBMS) or a NoSQL database based on your data structure and scalability needs.

3. Entity-Relationship Diagram (ERD):
   - Create an Entity-Relationship Diagram to model the entities, their attributes, and their relationships in the database. This visual representation helps you understand the structure of your data.

4. Normalize Your Data:
   - Normalize your data to minimize redundancy and improve data integrity. Follow normal forms (e.g., 1NF, 2NF, 3NF) to organize data efficiently.

5. Define Primary Keys and Foreign Keys:
   - Choose primary keys for each table to uniquely identify records. Use foreign keys to establish relationships between tables.

6. Choose Data Types:

- Select appropriate data types for each column to minimize storage and improve query performance. Common data types include integers, strings, dates, and floating-point numbers.

7. Indexing:
   - Use indexes for frequently queried columns to speed up data retrieval. Be cautious with over-indexing, as it can impact write performance.

8. Data Validation and Constraints:
   - Implement data validation and constraints to ensure data integrity and prevent data inconsistencies. Use check constraints, unique constraints, and foreign key constraints as needed.

9. Performance Considerations:
   - Optimize your database for performance by writing efficient SQL queries, creating appropriate indexes, and using caching when applicable.

10. Consider Scalability:
    - Plan for scalability from the beginning. Choose databases that can scale horizontally or vertically, depending on your needs. Employ techniques like load balancing and sharding.

11. Security Measures:
    - Implement strong security measures, including authentication, authorization, and encryption, to protect your database from unauthorized access and data breaches.

12. Error Handling:
    - Handle database errors gracefully by providing informative error messages and implementing retry mechanisms when applicable.

13. Document Your Design:

- Maintain thorough documentation of your database design, including the schema, tables, indexes, and constraints. This documentation is essential for team collaboration and future maintenance.

14. Testing and Validation:
    - Test your database design thoroughly to ensure that it meets the requirements and performs as expected. This includes validation of data integrity, data retrieval, and error handling.

15. Regular Backups and Recovery:
    - Establish a backup and recovery strategy to ensure data can be restored in case of data loss or corruption. Test the recovery process to validate its effectiveness.

16. Consider Data Privacy and Compliance:
    - Comply with data protection regulations and industry-specific compliance requirements (e.g., GDPR, HIPAA) to protect user data and ensure legal compliance.

17. Data Migration and Versioning:
    - Plan for data migration between database versions, especially in the case of schema changes or upgrades.

18. Disaster Recovery Plan:
    - Develop a disaster recovery plan that includes regular backups, redundancy, and geographic distribution for critical data.

19. Maintain Privacy:
    - Respect user privacy and secure sensitive information. Minimize data collection to only what is necessary for your application.

20. Monitor and Tune:

- Set up monitoring tools to track database performance, identify bottlenecks, and optimize queries, indexes, and database settings.

Effective database design is a foundational element of building reliable and scalable web applications. By following these best practices and principles, you can create a well-structured database system that ensures data integrity, optimizes performance, and meets the requirements of your web application.

Chapter 8: Web APIs and Security

Building and Securing Web APIs

Web APIs (Application Programming Interfaces) are a fundamental component of modern web applications, enabling communication and data exchange between different services and clients. In this chapter, we'll explore the process of building and securing web APIs.

1. Introduction to Web APIs:

Web APIs are endpoints that allow other software to interact with your application and request data or perform actions. They are crucial for enabling integration between different systems and platforms.

2. Designing Web APIs:

Effective API design is essential for providing a smooth developer experience and ensuring your API is easy to use and understand. Key considerations include:

- RESTful Design: Follow REST principles to create a well-structured API with meaningful endpoints, HTTP methods, and status codes.
- Versioning: Implement versioning to maintain backward compatibility when making changes to the API.
- Documentation: Provide comprehensive documentation that explains the purpose of each endpoint, required parameters, and expected responses.

3. Authentication and Authorization:

Securing your web API is critical to protect sensitive data and control access. Common methods for authentication and authorization include:

- API Keys: Assign unique keys to clients to authenticate their requests.
- OAuth: Implement OAuth for third-party authentication and authorization.
- JWT (JSON Web Tokens): Use JWT for token-based authentication and stateless authorization.
- Roles and Permissions: Define roles and permissions to control what actions users or clients can perform.

4. Input Validation:

Validate input data to prevent security vulnerabilities such as SQL injection and Cross-Site Scripting (XSS).

5. Rate Limiting:

Implement rate limiting to restrict the number of requests clients can make, preventing abuse and ensuring fair usage.

6. Cross-Origin Resource Sharing (CORS):

Use CORS headers to control which domains are allowed to make requests to your API.

7. Data Privacy:

Comply with data protection regulations and industry-specific compliance requirements (e.g., GDPR, HIPAA) to protect user data and ensure legal compliance.

8. Monitoring and Logging:

Set up monitoring and logging to track API usage, performance, and errors. Tools like New Relic and Datadog help monitor the health of your API.

9. API Versioning:

Plan for versioning your API to ensure backward compatibility as you make changes over time.

10. Rate Limiting and Throttling:

Implement rate limiting and request throttling to prevent abuse and ensure fair usage.

11. Secure File Uploads:

If your API allows file uploads, validate and sanitize uploaded files to prevent security vulnerabilities.

12. Testing and Validation:

Thoroughly test your API to ensure it meets requirements and performs as expected. This includes validating data integrity, data retrieval, and error handling.

13. Regular Security Audits:

Conduct security audits and penetration testing to identify and mitigate vulnerabilities.

14. Data Encryption:

Use encryption for sensitive data at rest and in transit. Employ protocols like HTTPS to secure data during transmission.

15. Disaster Recovery Plan:

Develop a disaster recovery plan that includes regular backups, redundancy, and geographic distribution for critical data.

16. Regular Security Updates:

Keep your API dependencies and libraries up to date to patch security vulnerabilities.

17. Compliance:

Comply with relevant industry and legal standards for data protection and security.

18. Security Education:

Train your development and operations teams in security best practices and provide guidelines for secure coding.

Conclusion:

Building and securing web APIs is essential for protecting sensitive data, ensuring fair usage, and providing a seamless experience for clients. By following best practices in API design, authentication, authorization, input validation, and monitoring, you can create secure and reliable APIs that meet the needs of your application and its users while also adhering to important data protection and privacy regulations.

Authentication and Authorization

Authentication and authorization are fundamental concepts in web development, especially when building secure web APIs and applications. These processes ensure that the right users or systems can access specific resources or perform certain actions. Let's dive into more technical details about authentication and authorization.

Authentication:

Authentication is the process of verifying the identity of a user, system, or entity trying to access a resource or perform an action within a web application. Here are some technical aspects of authentication:

User Credentials: Most commonly, authentication involves validating a user's identity through credentials, such as a username and password.

Token-Based Authentication: Token-based authentication is widely used for APIs and single-page applications. It involves issuing tokens (e.g., JSON Web Tokens or JWTs) upon successful login. The token is sent with each subsequent request, and the server verifies the token's authenticity and checks user permissions.

Multi-Factor Authentication (MFA): MFA adds an extra layer of security by requiring users to provide multiple forms of verification, such as a password and a one-time code sent to their mobile device.

OAuth and OpenID Connect: These protocols are often used for delegating authentication to third-party providers (e.g., social media logins) and single sign-on (SSO) solutions.

Session Management: In web applications, user sessions are established after successful authentication. Sessions are typically managed through cookies or tokens and are used to maintain user identity between requests.

Stateless Authentication: In stateless authentication, the server doesn't store session data, relying on tokens for validation. This approach is common in RESTful APIs and microservices.

Authentication Libraries: Frameworks like Passport.js for Node.js or Devise for Ruby on Rails provide pre-built tools for implementing authentication.

Authorization:

Authorization is the process of determining what actions or resources a user is allowed to access or modify after they have been authenticated. Here are technical aspects of authorization:

Role-Based Access Control (RBAC): In RBAC, users are assigned roles, and each role has a specific set of permissions. The server checks a user's role to decide if they can perform an action.

Attribute-Based Access Control (ABAC): ABAC considers various attributes, including user roles, resource attributes, and environmental conditions (e.g., time of day). This fine-grained approach is useful for complex authorization scenarios.

Policy-Based Authorization: Policies define rules for granting access based on specific conditions, and they can be expressed in code or configuration files.

Claims-Based Authorization: Claims are assertions about a user's identity, and they can be used to make authorization decisions. Claims are typically found in tokens issued during authentication.

Middleware and Filters: In web applications, middleware or filters can be applied to routes to check user permissions before allowing access. Frameworks like Express.js or ASP.NET offer middleware for this purpose.

API Key Authentication: For APIs, API keys are often used for authorization. The server checks the validity of the key before allowing access.

Token-Based Authorization: When working with APIs, tokens (e.g., OAuth tokens) can carry authorization information, including scopes or permissions, and are validated to determine access rights.

Database-Driven Authorization: Authorization rules can be stored in a database, allowing for dynamic changes without modifying the application code.

Access Control Lists (ACLs): ACLs provide a way to specify which users or groups can access or modify specific resources. ACLs are commonly used in file systems and some database systems.

Challenges and Best Practices:

- Least Privilege Principle: Follow the principle of least privilege, ensuring that users and systems have the minimum level of access required to perform their tasks.

- Token Security: Protect tokens from being stolen or intercepted. Implement token expiration and rotation policies.
- Secure Communication: Use HTTPS to secure data transmission and protect against man-in-the-middle attacks.
- Regular Auditing: Regularly audit your authentication and authorization mechanisms to identify and mitigate security risks.
- Data Validation: Ensure that input data is thoroughly validated to prevent security vulnerabilities.
- Authentication and Authorization Logging: Log authentication and authorization events for monitoring and security analysis.
- Education and Training: Train developers and administrators in best practices for authentication and authorization, as well as potential security threats.

Authentication and authorization are critical for securing web applications and APIs. Implementing these processes effectively is essential to protect user data, prevent unauthorized access, and maintain the integrity of your systems.

Chapter 9: Testing, Debugging, and Deployment

Testing Strategies

Testing, debugging, and deployment are essential stages in the software development lifecycle, ensuring the reliability and performance of your web application. Here, we'll delve into technical testing strategies and best practices.

1. Types of Testing:
- Unit Testing: Test individual components, functions, or methods in isolation to verify their correctness. Use testing frameworks like Jest, Mocha, or JUnit.
- Integration Testing: Verify the interactions between components or modules. Test how different parts of your application work together. Tools like Supertest or Postman can help with API integration testing.
- Functional Testing: Test the functionality of your application by interacting with it as a user would. Use tools like Selenium or Puppeteer for web application testing.
- End-to-End Testing (E2E): Test the entire application from end to end, simulating real user interactions. Frameworks like Cypress and Protractor are popular choices for E2E testing.
- Load and Performance Testing: Assess your application's performance under various load conditions. Tools like Apache JMeter or Gatling can simulate multiple users and concurrent requests.
- Security Testing: Identify vulnerabilities and weaknesses in your application through techniques

like penetration testing, security scanning, and code review.

2. Test Automation:

Automate as many tests as possible to ensure consistent and repeatable results. Use testing frameworks and libraries that support automation, such as Selenium WebDriver for web application testing or JUnit for Java applications.

3. Continuous Integration (CI) and Continuous Deployment (CD):

Integrate testing into your CI/CD pipeline. Automated tests should run on each code commit to identify and resolve issues early in the development process.

4. Test Data:

Use realistic and diverse test data to cover various scenarios. This includes using sample data, edge cases, and boundary conditions.

5. Mocking and Stubs:

Isolate components or services by using mocking or stubbing. Mock external services, databases, or APIs to ensure your tests focus solely on the functionality being tested.

6. Test Environments:

Maintain separate testing environments to simulate production conditions as closely as possible. These environments should mirror the actual infrastructure and configurations.

7. Regression Testing:

Perform regression testing to ensure that new changes do not introduce new defects or break existing functionality.

8. Code Coverage:

Measure code coverage to ensure your tests exercise a sufficient portion of your codebase. Tools like Istanbul for JavaScript or Jacoco for Java can help track code coverage.

9. Test Reporting:

Generate detailed test reports that provide information on test results and code coverage. This helps identify areas that require improvement.

10. Debugging:

- Use debugging tools and techniques to identify and resolve issues during development and testing. Browser developer tools, IDE debuggers, and logging are valuable for this purpose.

11. Deployment:

- Deploy your application to production in a controlled and systematic manner, following these deployment best practices:
- Continuous Deployment: Automate the deployment process to reduce the risk of human error. Tools like Jenkins, Travis CI, or GitHub Actions can help with continuous deployment.
- Staging Environments: Before deploying to production, thoroughly test changes in a staging environment that closely mirrors the production environment.
- Rollback Strategies: Have rollback procedures in place in case an issue arises during deployment. This ensures a quick return to a stable state.
- Blue-Green Deployment: Implement blue-green deployment to switch between two identical environments (one for production and one for deployment) to minimize downtime and risk.

- Canary Releases: Gradually roll out changes to a subset of users or servers to monitor and mitigate any unforeseen issues.

12. Monitoring:
    - Use monitoring tools like New Relic, Datadog, or Prometheus to keep an eye on the health and performance of your application in production. Monitor key metrics and set up alerts for potential issues.

13. Rollout and Scaling:
    - As your application grows, ensure your deployment strategy supports scaling horizontally and vertically to handle increased traffic and load.

14. Version Control:
    - Utilize version control systems like Git to manage your application's codebase. Keep code in a repository and use branches for feature development and bug fixes.

15. Testing in Production:
    - Implement feature flags or dark launches to test new functionality in a production environment while keeping it hidden from users.

Technical testing, debugging, and deployment are crucial aspects of delivering a reliable and high-performance web application. By applying the right testing strategies, automating tests, and following deployment best practices, you can ensure the quality and stability of your software.

Chapter 10: Emerging Web Technologies

WebAssembly, PWAs, and More

Emerging web technologies continue to shape the landscape of web development, providing new tools and capabilities to build faster, more feature-rich, and more interactive web applications. In this technical overview, we'll delve into some of these emerging technologies, including WebAssembly (Wasm), Progressive Web Apps (PWAs), and more.

1. WebAssembly (Wasm):

Technical Overview:

- WebAssembly (Wasm) is a binary instruction format that allows high-performance execution of code in web browsers. It's a low-level virtual machine that is designed to run code written in languages like C, C++, and Rust, alongside JavaScript.

Use Cases:

- High-Performance Web Apps: Wasm enables computationally intensive tasks like video editing, gaming, and scientific simulations to run in web browsers with near-native performance.
- Porting Existing Code: It allows developers to port existing codebases written in languages other than JavaScript to run in browsers.
- Augmented Reality (AR) and Virtual Reality (VR): Wasm can enhance the performance of AR and VR applications in the browser.

2. Progressive Web Apps (PWAs):

Technical Overview:

- Progressive Web Apps (PWAs) are web applications that leverage modern web technologies to provide an app-like experience on the web. They are built with a set of technologies and design patterns that enhance user engagement and performance.

Key Features:

- Service Workers: These scripts run in the background, intercept network requests, and enable features like offline access, push notifications, and background sync.
- Web App Manifest: A JSON file that provides metadata about the web app, allowing users to install it on their device's home screen.
- HTTPS: PWAs require a secure connection (HTTPS) to ensure data privacy and security.

Use Cases:

- Offline Access: PWAs work even when the network connection is unreliable or non-existent.
- Cross-Platform: They can be accessed on various devices and platforms without the need for native app stores.
- Improved Performance: PWAs load quickly and provide a smooth user experience.

3. WebRTC (Web Real-Time Communication):

Technical Overview:

- WebRTC is a collection of APIs and protocols that enable real-time communication in web browsers without the need for plugins or native applications.

Key Features:

- Peer-to-Peer Communication: WebRTC allows direct communication between browsers, making it

suitable for video chat, voice calling, and file sharing.
- Data Channels: Developers can create peer-to-peer data channels for exchanging arbitrary data.
- NAT and Firewall Traversal: WebRTC is designed to work in various network environments, including those with NAT and firewall restrictions.

Use Cases:
- Video Conferencing: WebRTC powers video conferencing applications and services.
- Live Streaming: It's used for live streaming video and audio.
- Gaming: WebRTC enables real-time multiplayer games in web browsers.

4. Web Components:

Technical Overview:
- Web Components are a set of web platform APIs that allow developers to create reusable and encapsulated custom HTML elements.

Key Features:
- Custom Elements: Define your own HTML elements with encapsulated CSS and JavaScript.
- Shadow DOM: Isolate the CSS and JavaScript of a custom element from the rest of the page to prevent conflicts.
- Templates: Create reusable templates that can be stamped out into instances of custom elements.

Use Cases:
- Reusability: Web components promote code reusability by encapsulating functionality and design in custom elements.

- Interoperability: They work well with existing web technologies and frameworks.

5. GraphQL:

Technical Overview:

- GraphQL is a query language for your API and a server-side runtime for executing those queries by using a type system that you define for your data.

Key Features:

- Client-Defined Queries: Clients can request exactly the data they need, reducing over-fetching or under-fetching of data.
- Real-time Data: GraphQL can be used to create real-time data subscriptions.
- Strong Typing: The type system provides a clear contract for the data.

Use Cases:

- Flexible APIs: GraphQL is ideal for APIs that need to be flexible and support various clients with different data requirements.
- Single Endpoint: It allows multiple data sources to be accessed through a single API endpoint.

These emerging web technologies offer exciting possibilities for web developers, enabling them to create faster, more powerful, and more engaging web applications. By staying up-to-date with these technologies and mastering their technical details, you can take full advantage of the latest tools and capabilities in web development.

Best Practices and Conclusion

Code Quality

Code Linting:

- Utilize code linters like ESLint, JSHint, or TSLint to enforce coding standards. Configure linters to your project's specific requirements, and integrate them into your development workflow.

Static Code Analysis:

- Employ static code analysis tools like SonarQube or ESLint to automatically detect issues such as code smells, security vulnerabilities, and maintainability concerns.

Continuous Integration and Continuous Deployment (CI/CD):

- Automate the code quality checks in your CI/CD pipeline. Integrate code analysis, unit tests, and other quality checks to prevent low-quality code from reaching production.

Test Automation:

- Ensure comprehensive test coverage, including unit, integration, and end-to-end tests. Use testing frameworks like Jest, Mocha, or Selenium, and leverage testing libraries to simulate user interactions.

Code Reviews with Tools:

- Use code review tools like GitHub, GitLab, or Bitbucket to streamline the code review process. These platforms provide code diff highlighting and commenting features.

Automated Code Formatting:

- Implement code formatting tools like Prettier or Black (for Python) to maintain consistent code style automatically.

Collaboration:

Git Branching Strategy:

- Define a Git branching strategy that suits your project's needs. Common strategies include Git Flow, Feature Branching, and GitHub Flow.

Merge and Pull Request Workflow:

- Follow a merge or pull request workflow where code changes are reviewed and approved before merging into the main branch. Use tools like GitHub or GitLab for this purpose.

Continuous Integration (CI) Integration:

- Configure your CI server to automatically build and test code changes in branches or pull requests. This ensures that proposed changes are functional.

Issue Tracking and Agile Methodologies:

- Utilize issue tracking systems such as Jira or Asana to manage tasks and user stories. Adopt agile methodologies like Scrum or Kanban for project management.

Collaboration Platforms:

- Leverage collaboration platforms like Slack, Microsoft Teams, or Discord for real-time communication and file sharing among team members.

Knowledge Sharing:

- Establish a knowledge-sharing culture within your team. Encourage team members to document code, processes, and solutions in a central knowledge base or a wiki.

Code Ownership:

- Clearly define code ownership and responsibilities. Assign code maintainers for different parts of the project to ensure accountability.

Significance:

- From a technical perspective, code quality and collaboration practices are integral to the development process. Code quality tools, continuous integration, and test automation ensure that the software is robust and reliable.
- Collaborative practices, including Git workflows, code reviews, and issue tracking, create a structured and efficient development environment. Effective communication tools and knowledge sharing lead to a cohesive team.

In summary, a focus on code quality and collaboration is fundamental in delivering high-quality web applications. By integrating these practices into the technical aspects of web development, you can produce maintainable and reliable software while promoting efficient teamwork.

Staying Current in Web Development

Web development is an ever-evolving field, characterized by rapid advancements in technologies, tools, and best practices. To remain effective and competitive, web developers must stay current with the latest trends and innovations. In this technical view, we'll explore strategies and techniques for staying current in web development.

1. Continuous Learning:

Web developers must embrace a culture of continuous learning. The rapid pace of technological change demands a commitment to staying up-to-date with new tools and practices. Here's how to do it:

- Online Courses and Tutorials: Enroll in online courses and tutorials on platforms like Coursera, edX, and Pluralsight. Courses often cover cutting-edge technologies and provide hands-on experience.
- Technical Blogs: Follow technical blogs and news sites like Smashing Magazine, CSS-Tricks, and A List Apart. These sources provide in-depth insights into the latest web development trends and techniques.
- YouTube and Webinars: YouTube channels and webinars hosted by experts are excellent resources for learning new skills. Channels like Traversy Media and The Net Ninja offer comprehensive tutorials on various web development topics.
- Conferences and Meetups: Attend web development conferences, workshops, and local meetups. Events like Google I/O, Web Summit, and Smashing Conf provide opportunities to learn, network, and gain practical insights.
- Books and Documentation: Consult documentation and web development books. The MDN Web Docs is an invaluable resource for understanding web technologies.

- MOOCs and Self-Paced Learning: Explore Massive Open Online Courses (MOOCs) from universities and self-paced learning platforms like Udacity and Udemy. These platforms offer specialized courses on web development topics.

2. Experimentation and Personal Projects:

Practical experience is essential for mastering new web development technologies. Developers can keep current by working on personal projects and experimentation:

- Side Projects: Create side projects to explore new technologies and put your learning into practice. Choose projects that align with your interests, from building a personal blog to creating web applications.
- Open Source Contribution: Contribute to open-source projects. This not only enhances your skillset but also allows you to collaborate with experienced developers and make a meaningful impact on the community.
- CodePen and GitHub Gists: Platforms like CodePen and GitHub Gists are excellent for quick experimentation and sharing code snippets.
- Prototyping: Use prototyping tools like Figma and Adobe XD to design and prototype web interfaces and interactions.

3. Version Control and Package Management:

Web development tools and libraries are frequently updated. Managing dependencies and tracking changes is crucial to staying current:

- Version Control: Utilize Git for version control to track code changes and collaborate with others.

Platforms like GitHub and GitLab facilitate team collaboration and code review.

- Package Managers: Use package managers like npm for JavaScript and Composer for PHP to manage and update dependencies efficiently.
- Semver: Understand Semantic Versioning (Semver) to interpret version numbers and decide on updating dependencies.

4. Frameworks and Libraries:

Web development frameworks and libraries evolve rapidly. It's essential to monitor their updates and adapt as necessary:

- JavaScript Frameworks: Keep current with popular JavaScript frameworks such as React, Angular, and Vue.js. Follow their official documentation and release notes.
- CSS Frameworks: Stay informed about CSS frameworks like Bootstrap, Foundation, and Materialize to leverage their latest features.
- Library Ecosystem: Explore JavaScript libraries and extensions. For example, explore the vibrant ecosystem of npm packages and tools like Webpack and Babel.

5. Browser and Device Compatibility:

Web developers must ensure their websites and applications work seamlessly across various browsers and devices:

- Browser Developer Tools: Master browser developer tools like Chrome DevTools and Firefox Developer Tools to diagnose and debug compatibility issues.

- Cross-Browser Testing: Utilize cross-browser testing tools such as BrowserStack, CrossBrowserTesting, or Sauce Labs to test your websites on various browsers and devices.

6. Web Performance and Optimization:

Staying current in web development involves optimizing websites for performance, user experience, and search engine rankings:

- Performance Tools: Learn to use performance measurement tools like Lighthouse, PageSpeed Insights, and GTmetrix to identify and address performance bottlenecks.
- Progressive Web Apps (PWAs): Explore PWAs to create fast, reliable, and engaging web applications. Understand service workers, app manifest files, and responsive design practices.

7. Security Best Practices:

Staying current also means staying updated on the latest security vulnerabilities and best practices:

- Security News: Subscribe to security news sources like OWASP, Hacker News, and security blogs to stay informed about the latest threats and mitigation techniques.
- Security Tools: Employ security testing tools like OWASP ZAP, Burp Suite, and Acunetix to identify vulnerabilities in your web applications.

8. Web APIs and Microservices:

The web is moving towards a more API-driven architecture. Keeping current in this area is crucial:

- RESTful APIs: Learn about creating and consuming RESTful APIs, understanding HTTP methods, and implementing best practices.

- GraphQL: Explore the benefits of GraphQL and how to create flexible and efficient APIs.
- Microservices: Understand microservices architecture and its role in web development, including containerization with Docker and orchestration with Kubernetes.

9. Automation and DevOps:

Automation and DevOps practices are essential for web development teams. Stay current with automation and continuous integration:

- CI/CD: Implement Continuous Integration and Continuous Deployment (CI/CD) pipelines using tools like Jenkins, Travis CI, and GitLab CI/CD.
- Infrastructure as Code (IaC): Explore IaC tools like Terraform and Ansible to automate infrastructure provisioning and management.

10. Augmented and Virtual Reality (AR/VR):

Augmented and virtual reality are emerging technologies that can impact web development:

- WebAR and WebVR: Explore WebAR and WebVR to create immersive web experiences using technologies like A-Frame and Three.js.

11. Web Accessibility:

Web accessibility is an essential consideration, and staying current involves keeping up with accessibility standards and best practices:

- WCAG: Understand the Web Content Accessibility Guidelines (WCAG) and how to make web content more accessible to individuals with disabilities.

Conclusion:

Staying current in web development is a continuous journey. It involves learning new technologies, adapting to evolving best practices, and staying informed about emerging trends. As the web development landscape evolves, web developers who invest in continuous learning and practical application will remain competitive and deliver high-quality web solutions. By following these technical strategies, developers can ensure that their skills and knowledge are always up to date in this dynamic field

Appendix: Resources

Useful Websites, Books, and Tools

1. Useful Websites:
   - MDN Web Docs (developer.mozilla.org): A comprehensive resource for web development, offering documentation on HTML, CSS, JavaScript, and more.
   - W3Schools (w3schools.com): A beginner-friendly website providing tutorials and references on web technologies.
   - Stack Overflow (stackoverflow.com): A vibrant community of developers sharing knowledge and helping with coding challenges.
   - CSS-Tricks (css-tricks.com): A source for CSS tips, tricks, and guides.
   - GitHub (github.com): A platform for hosting and collaborating on code projects. It's essential for version control and open-source contributions.

2. Recommended Books:
   - "Eloquent JavaScript" by Marijn Haverbeke: A comprehensive book for mastering JavaScript, a fundamental language for web development.
   - "CSS Secrets" by Lea Verou: Explores advanced CSS techniques and best practices.
   - "You Don't Know JS" (book series) by Kyle Simpson: A series of books that delves deep into JavaScript's intricacies.
   - "Learning Web Design" by Jennifer Niederst Robbins: An excellent starting point for beginners covering HTML, CSS, and web design principles.

- "Node.js Design Patterns" by Mario Casciaro: A guide to applying design patterns in Node.js development.

3. Essential Tools:
- Visual Studio Code (code.visualstudio.com): A free, open-source code editor highly customizable and packed with extensions for web development.
- Git (git-scm.com): A distributed version control system for tracking changes in source code.
- GitHub (github.com): A platform for hosting, sharing, and collaborating on Git repositories.
- Browser Developer Tools: Learn how to use the built-in tools in browsers like Chrome and Firefox for debugging and inspecting web pages.
- CodePen (codepen.io): An online community for testing and showcasing HTML, CSS, and JavaScript code snippets.

www.ingramcontent.com/pod-product-compliance
Lightning Source LLC
Chambersburg PA
CBHW060951260726
48661CB00005B/1836